Creating Space

38 Strategies to Help You Make Time for What's Important

Jennifer,
Create Wonderful Spaces!
Diana

Creating Space

A Weston Lyon & Diana Fletcher Book

Book Cover created by Melanie DePaoli
(Owner of Omicle)

Book Edited by Debbie Fletcher
(Diana's awesome sister)

ISBN: 1438206356

Our Personal Thanks to...

"For all their love, support and encouragement, I want to thank my husband **Eric**, my children, **Michael**, **Rachel** and **Amanda**, and my family and friends. I want to thank Weston Lyon for being such a great writing partner. I especially want to thank my sister, **Cindy**, who never doubted that I would do this."

-Diana

"First, I want to thank **David L. Holzer** for teaching me how to "time block". Without his help this book wouldn't exist. Second, I want to thank my mentors: **Matt Furey, Dan Kennedy, Bill Glazier, Becky Gomes, & Ali Brown**. They've laid the ground work for me and for that I'm grateful. Last, I want to thank **Diana Fletcher** for making this book easy and *enjoyable* to write."

-Weston

Creating Space

38 Strategies:

Table of Contents

1. Time Blocking

2. Plan Your Day

3. It's ONLY 15 Minutes

4. What Should I Wear?!!!?

5. Procrastination is a Killer

6. Important, NOT Urgent

7. Learn to be Lazy

8. Demand It!

9. Super Size It for Later

10. Step Away from the Phone

11. Wonderful, Glorious Breakfast!

12. Once and For All, Set up Your Work Areas

13. Get off the Computer

14. E-mail and S&R Disorder

15. Do Not Read Every E-mail

16. Plan Your Errands

17. It's OK to Say No

18. A Place for Everything and Everything in Its Place

19. Exercise at Home

20. Exercise with Your Children

21. Get Help!

22. Ask for Help!

23. Leverage OPT

24. Enjoy Customer Service

25. Children and How to Use Them

26. TEAMwork at Work

27. Stop Accepting Every Invitation

28. Plan Meetings During Lunch or Walks

29. Surprise! You Have to Eat Everyday!

30. Keep Healthy Food Handy

31. The Wonder of Notebooks and Lists

32. Stop Perfecting

33. Quick Decisions

34. Stop Talking

35. Television: The Sneaky Time Stealer

36. Overestimate Your Time

37. Welcome the Spaces that are Being Created for You

38. How are You Spending Your Days?

Introduction

Have you ever said to yourself, "So much to do...and no time to get it all done?"

I bet you have a lot of "to do's" in your life. You have so much to get done, but it feels like time just keeps on ticking.

I assure you time will not stop – though we all wish it did at times. We all have a finite amount of time every week. So how do some people get more done than others? How do some people seem to move through life with ease, while others struggle?

Diana and I are not going to tell you we have all the answers...we wish we did, but we don't. What we can tell you is this:

 Life is not about _doing_
Life is about _living_!

Now, each and every one of us has a different outlook on life. We all value life's delights in a different way. And we all prioritize those delights in order of importance.

That's why Diana and I wrote this book. We realize life is about living. We realize life is about what's important. And the problem most of us face is:

We don't have the time for what's important!?!

This book is the key to creating that time. This book will give you strategies on how to make time – for what's important in YOUR life.

Are you ready? *Let's get started!*

Weston Lyon
Author, Speaker, &
KING of the Functional Fitness Jungle

Diana Fletcher
Author, Speaker, &
TotalHealth Coach

How to Use This Book

We have designed our book, <u>Creating Space</u>, as a quick resource for ideas to create space for what is truly important, each and every day.

As you read <u>Creating Space</u>, highlight or underline the ideas that make sense in your life. Circle the actions that you feel would be manageable for you.

There are many different ideas and not all of them will work for everyone. At this point, you want to concentrate on what would work *for you*, right now.

There are so many great ideas, that you will end up circling many that you could use. When you finish reading, go back through and pick *three* of your favorite ideas and list them here:

1. _____

2. _____

3. _____

Now pick one action to begin with **right now.** This will be your first action and we urge you to give it at least one week to see how it works in your life.

If it works, keep doing it. If you have trouble with it, examine your attempt/action a little closer. Are you honestly giving it a chance? Are you putting up roadblocks or truly trying to create space?

After examining it, if you really think that this action will not work for you, go on to another idea.

Once you have incorporated one new action into your life and are seeing the results, you are ready to go on to your next action. You may want to add a new action each week, or every two weeks.

Once you see the amazing results that come from creating space in your life, go back through the book and take on a few more ideas.

You may even start thinking of your own ways to create more space in your life. If you do let us know...we'd love to hear from you!

By takings these actions, you will notice less stress and more happiness in your life. By creating space, you are opening yourself up to amazing and wonderful possibilities for a truly *Outstanding Life.*

Creating Space

Time Blocking

The sculpture is already inside the stone.

Michelangelo

Time blocking changed my life. I remember talking to a mentor of mine, David L. Holzer, about not being able to have the time to write my first book, <u>USE IT TO LOSE IT.</u>

He asked me, *"Have you ever used time blocking?"*

"What is time blocking?" I questioned.

David said, *"Time blocking is when you sit down with your schedule and block out x amount of time to do a project of importance. For example, if you want to write your book faster, block out 3-4 hours once a week. That way you know when you're going to write."*

"That's genius!" I said.

You see, I had good intentions of writing my book in a timely manner. However, every time I wanted to write, something else got in the way.

With time blocking I was able to knock out my first book in less than 60 days. How do you start blocking? Here's how:

1. Choose an activity that is important to you

2. Take out your schedule and block out the amount of time you want to dedicate to this activity

3. Make a commitment to yourself to NEVER give this time to anyone or anything else

It's really that simple. Try it now with one activity of importance. Then use time blocking for the other activities that are important in your life.

Here are some examples of what I use time blocking for:

- **Exercise**
- **Writing**
- **Meeting with clients**
- **Meeting with referral partners**
- **Meetings in general**
- **Playing with my son, Haven**
- **Relaxing**
- **Getting a massage**
- **Spending time with my family**
- **Martial arts practice**

The list goes on and on. I started with my writing time to finish my first book. Now, I time block everything!

Plan Your Day

It is the choices you make today
that are creating...your future.

Shad Helmstetter

Not only do you want to start blocking your time...you also want to start planning your time.

Every night before you go to bed (or before you leave work) look at your schedule for the next day. Take the following steps to plan your next day for success:

1. Write down 5 things you feel are important to get done

2. Prioritize them in the order they need to get done (1 being the most important and 5 being the least important)

3. Block time for your first 3 items

Now, when you wake up (or get to work) make sure you review this list one more time, so you know what you're doing. Here's what to do next:

1. Act on your #1 priority until it's DONE!
2. Then and only then move to priority numero dos
3. Then and only then move to priority numero tres

If you get done with your first 3 priorities,

Most people never accomplish that much important stuff in one day. Now, move onto priorities four and five. Get those done and you're going to be unstoppable.

Do this every day and watch how much more you get done.

It's ONLY
15 Minutes

I have always been delighted at the prospect
of a new day, a fresh try, one more start, with
perhaps a bit of magic waiting somewhere
behind the morning.

J. B. Priestley

I know this may sound like a pain, but it works wonders.

If you like the morning already, get up an extra 15 minutes early. The house will be quiet. You can have time to think, exercise, or go to the bathroom (peacefully, without kids knocking on the door).

If like me, you're not a morning person, go to bed 15 minutes later than usual. You won't miss that extra sleep and you'll be amazed at how much you can get done in 15 minutes when no one is bothering you.

Notice the underlying theme here: **uninterrupted time**.

You have the ability to get so much done when you can work (or relax) without interruption. The key here is to know yourself and take action on what works best for you.

Are you an early riser? Wake up earlier!
Are you a night owl? Go to bed later!

(Note: For 100 Things to Do in Fifteen Minutes, go to Diana's website: **www.dianafletcher.com**)

Diana Fletcher & Weston Lyon

23

Creating Space

What Should I Wear?!!?

Life can be challenging...
dressing should not be.

Susan Grave

All right, just so you know, this topic is not just for women. It's for men, women and children.

Why are we so confused in the morning about clothes? Every day, we have to get dressed. Every day we have to decide what to wear, based on where we will be and what we will be doing. Still, we wait until morning, staring in a stupor at the clothes hanging in our closet, wondering what we should put on.

The typical morning for many people goes like this:

✓Where is my (*fill in the blank*)?
✓Is my (*fill in the blank*) clean/ironed/still in existence?
✓Do I have the sock that matches this one?
✓Where did I leave my (*fill in the blank*)?

Sometimes we are asking ourselves this question, sometimes other people, much to their annoyance.

All of this stress and time wasting could be avoided by planning ahead. If you do not have time on the weekend to do much more than get laundry caught up or pick up the dry cleaning, you could at least prepare each night for the next day.

Even if all you wear are jeans, tee shirts, or work-out clothes, it can make your whole morning routine go much more smoothly.

Having everything laid out, clean, ironed and organized, can be so calming in the morning. Children benefit from doing this just as much as adults. (Warning: Teen-age boys will laugh at you if you suggest this.)

Starting the day this way can create a huge difference in your morning. You will feel the benefit of creating this space when you realize that you have time for breakfast or a cup of coffee *sitting down*!

Creating Space

Procrastination is a Killer

Success is waiting for you
to make the first move.

John Maxwell

Okay, I admit it...I love to procrastinate. It's human nature to do so. However, procrastinating will kill your chances at an outstanding life.

This is what happens when you procrastinate:

First, you delay your success. For example, if you put off writing down what's important in your life you'll delay your success in achieving it.

It doesn't mean you won't have success. It means you'll have to wait longer to get it.

Second, you set yourself up to feel rushed and then stressed. For example, if you put off getting gas in your car, you'll feel stressed out when you have to be somewhere and need to get gas (before you have to walk).

I've been in this situation before. It sucks.

Third, you condition yourself to keep putting things off. This is probably the worst of the three. When you procrastinate once and get the job done anyway, you condition yourself to keep procrastinating because you know you can get the job done again.

This conditioning creates a never-ending cycle. If you get caught in the cycle, life will not be very fun.

So, how do you get over procrastination?

You decide to take action now!

That's it. It's simple, but it's the truth. I made this decision a few years ago, and it's been one of the best decisions of my life.

It's your turn. Make the decision to take action on whatever you have at hand. Do it. Get it done. Succeed. And break the habit of procrastination once and for all.

(Note: You don't want to take action on every "to do" in your life. Just the important tasks. Let's cover that next...)

Important, NOT Urgent

Either you run the day or the day runs you.

J.C. McPheeters

If you want to take stress out of your life and make life more fulfilling, you MUST learn the difference between things being *important* and *urgent,* and how to harmonize them.

No offense to Webster, but here are my definitions in terms of actions to be taken:

Important – actions that get you closer to your desired result

Urgent – actions that need to be done immediately

Okay, let's first take a look at the difference between them. Important actions get you closer to your desired result. Isn't that what life is all about – achieving results you want to happen.

On the other hand, urgent actions need to be done immediately. Now, they may be important too; however, urgent actions won't get you any closer to your desired result. In fact, most actions that are urgent take you away from your desired result and closer to someone else's desired result.

So how do we harmonize them?

First, you need to know what you want.

Second, you need to be committed to what you want.

Finally, you need to be flexible.

Like I said before, life happens. It's unfortunate, but people die, hearts get broken, and so on. Here's a common sense example of how to harmonize:

You're getting ready to go exercise (because it's really important) and you get a phone call from your best friend.

His/her significant other just broke his/her heart. What do you do? Go work out and call your friend later *or* get your butt over to comfort them?

You go work out...just kidding!

Of course you go comfort your friend. It's not important (by the definition above), but it is certainly urgent.

Go to your friend now and work out later. Listen, your friend needs you now – urgent. Your body needs exercise sometime that day – important. Just work out later and you'll be good to go.

That's being flexible. **You're urgent in crisis, but NOT just for the hell of it.** Take action on important items 90-95% of the time and you'll be well on your way.

(Note: Your friendships may rank higher in importance than your health. If that's the case, then the situation above would not only be urgent, it would be important too (by the definition I gave you))

Learn to be Lazy

I make no secret of the fact that I
would rather lie on a sofa than sweep
beneath it. But you have to be efficient
if you're going to be lazy.

Shirley Conran

We talked about important vs. urgent. Now, let's look at *important* vs. *unimportant*.

If important actions get you closer to your desired result, then unimportant actions get you nowhere near your desired result.

So my solution is: **Learn to be lazy!**

I don't mean be a bum. I mean learn to be lazy about activities that don't really matter in life. Actions that don't get you what you really want.

Here's a list of the tasks that are *unimportant* in my life:

- **Washing dishes**
- **Cutting grass**
- **Washing my car**
- **Cleaning my house**
- **Organizing my desk**
- **And much, much more**

I hate doing these chores. They are NOT getting me any closer to the results I want. Therefore, I don't do them...or I'm lazy at doing them.

I wait until the last possible minute to do some of them, and others I give to someone else to do.

It's not because I can't. It's because I'd rather spend my time here on this planet taking action on the things I want to do!

Learning to be lazy will help you create space in your life for your desired results. What are some things you could learn to be lazy about? List them here:

1. _____

2. _____

3. _____

Creating Space

Demand It!

The secret to getting absolutely anything you want is simple: do whatever it takes.

Mike Hernacki

State your demands, first to yourself and then to others. Make creating space for an outstanding life a priority. You have to totally embrace the idea that you are important and that your time, your desires, and your needs are important.

Until you insist on this, nothing will change.

People are very busy with their own lives. The people you live with, your co-workers and your friends are all busy.

Even the people closest to you are not going to be thinking of your needs every day. It is up to you to make your wishes known and stick to your guns.

Tell yourself that you will have time every single day. It does not matter if you believe this right away. Once you start changing your thoughts, your brain will start making the thoughts come true.

You will discover opportunities and come up with all sorts of ideas to help you find time.

People may not understand it, but they will begin to respect it. They may not like it, but everyone will benefit from it.

Your children will have a clear example of how to take care of themselves. You will be rested and healthier and able to accomplish everything you want to accomplish each day.

You will be on your way to living an outstanding life!

Creating Space

Super Size It for Later

"Would you like to super size that?"

Any fast food employee

If you are going to put in the work and the time, double what you do. For example, when you cook, make double the amount. Freeze the other half and you have created extra space in your life.

How nice would that be to open your freezer in the morning, transfer the evening meal to your refrigerator and let it defrost while you are working?

And about that meal prep...how about doubling the help? An extra person helping with just a few tasks in the kitchen can make the preparation time so much shorter!

 Even a young child can set the table and older ones can take out pans and be "your assistant."

When you make a salad, make enough to have for the next day's lunch. Instant healthy lunch—no prep time in the morning!

Another way of creating space in your life is to double the amounts you buy. If your budget allows it, buying ahead can help create time later.

Buying double the paper products, toiletries, and food staples that you know you always need, saves that last minute running to the store.

The idea is to create space, slow down, and make your time really matter. Because it does!

Step Away from the Phone

Often short term gain
produces long term pain.

Anonymous

We've all been conditioned to answer the phone as soon as we hear it ring.

My son, who's only 5 years old, is already conditioned to do this. Why? Because he sees the grown-ups around him race for the phone as soon as they hear it like a dog chasing a fake rabbit at the track.

We have a big family so my son gets to experience a lot of different environments. When he's with me, I try to break him of this habit.

Why?

Because having the habit of always answering the phone when it rings creates problems in your life. Here are a few problems to keep in mind:

 Answering the phone can interrupt your thoughts

If you're brainstorming or daydreaming don't answer the phone! Your thoughts are way more important than whoever is on the end of the line. If you're meditating, turn the phone off. Silence is golden.

Answering the phone takes time away from important tasks

If you're in the middle of something important, don't answer the phone! An important task takes precedence over any phone call.

 Answering the phone can drain your energy

This may sound silly, but the person on the other end may drain your energy. Maybe it's a telemarketer who makes you angry. Maybe it's a family member asking for money (like that's never happened to you). Whatever the case may be, don't let this happen to you.

Final thoughts: Step away from the phone and enjoy what you're doing in the moment. If you are expecting an important call, at least have Caller ID to make sure it's the right person.

Everyone can leave a message. It's no big deal. They would anyway if you weren't home.

Wonderful, Glorious Breakfast!

Prior planning prevents poor performance.

Anonymous

Here's an interesting one. By eating breakfast, you can create space in your day. At first, this may not make sense. It seems that you are adding something to do, so how can this create space? Let me explain.

It's our most important meal of the day, and what do we do? We forget to eat it, we eat it on the run, or, let's face it, we eat garbage. (Yes, donuts, sweet rolls and fast food breakfasts are garbage. I'm sorry. I had to say it.)

Breakfast is the meal that gives you your fuel for the day. This is the meal that can set the tone for your mood and how you approach your work and your life. It breaks your fast and keeps your blood sugar levels balanced if done properly. And this is often the meal we ignore.

All right. You may already be eating breakfast everyday and you may even be eating a healthy breakfast every day. Bravo! Keep up the good work!

However if you're not, this is a very important space creator for your day that you are missing out on.

Planning ahead and taking the time to sit down and eat a proper breakfast, enables you to avoid the mid-morning hunger attack – when your energy levels are low.

If you're losing time because you're feeling drowsy, having brain fog, or just daydreaming, then this is important for you to take action on immediately.

Creating Space

Once and For All, Set Up Your Work Areas

Short as life is, we make it still shorter
by the careless waste of time.

Victor Hugo

How much time do you spend looking for what you need every time you start a project or task? What a waste of time!

You go to do some cleaning, and you left your supplies in another room. You are ready to start a job fixing something, and you cannot find the tools you need to start, let alone finish. You go into your office and nothing is where you thought you left it.

At this point, you look at the clock and realize that by the time you assemble everything you need, you will be late, rushed, or unable to finish, yet again.

Stop. It's time to get organized. Break the organizing into small steps and do it once and for all.

Think of the trouble spots. Where do you get slowed down the most? Housework, household repairs, paperwork?

Start with the one that bothers you the most, and go to that area. Make a list of all the supplies you need. If the supplies are in the house, assemble them.

Assembling may take time, but keep at it until you are done. Make a plan to go to the store and get everything else to fill in the gaps. While you are there, buy containers and boxes to hold the supplies.

Keep them in the same place, all the time with warnings like DO NOT TOUCH if you anticipate problems. (My children always take my tape and scissors. I now hide them.)

If you are overwhelmed, there are professional organizers who do this work. They are able to help you "zero in" on the trouble spots and give you good, solid suggestions on how to become more organized.

Once you have your tools in place for all projects, you will save huge amounts of time. More time for healthier living!

Get off the Computer

If you keep doing that...you'll go blind!

Anonymous

I'm guilty myself at times, but we have to learn to get off the computer.

We use the computer at home. We use the computer at work. Heck, I've even used my laptop in the bathroom when I was swamped and needed a quiet space (embarrassing, but true).

Here's what to do so you can create more space in your life...without the computer.

1. Buy a digital timer. (They're cheap.)

2. Put it beside you when you're on the computer and make sure you activate it.

3. Notice and write down how much time you spend with this inanimate object, your computer.

I guarantee that it will surprise you at first. What surprised me the most was how much time I was spending checking e-mail. (We'll get to this next.)

Now that you know how much time you're spending in front of the computer do this:

Make a list of activities that take the same amount of time.

For example, if you spend 2 hours in front a computer every day, what activity can you do in that same amount of time?

✓ Can you go exercise instead?

✓ Can you continue reading your favorite novel?

✓ Can you spend time with your wife, husband, or significant other?

✓ Can you enjoy time with your kids?

What can YOU do with that time?

You probably won't be able to get away from your computer for the entire amount of time, but you will be able to cut back and enjoy life more now that you know this.

Now, let's conquer e-mail...

E-mail and
S&R Disorder

All our lauded technological progress – our
very civilization – is like the axe in the hand
of the pathological criminal.

Albert Einstein

I'm convinced e-mail is evil.

It's the biggest time waster we have today. In fact, it's even responsible for a new disorder that has developed over the past 10 years...

It's called S&R Disorder. Or more common called Send & Receive Disorder(thank you Ali Brown for alerting me to this disorder).

Here's how to diagnose it:

- If you have e-mail alerts every time an e-mail is sent to you...*you have S&R Disorder*

- If you check your e-mail first thing in the morning...*you have S&R Disorder*

- If you check your e-mails every time you walk in the room...*you have S&R Disorder*

This disorder is unfortunately common today. Hundreds of millions of people from around the globe have already been affected by this disorder.

Don't be another statistic! Take action. Here's how I saved myself from "*e-mail the evil*":

1. I disabled the feature that allows e-mail to flow into my computer without my knowledge, as well as the "alert" to new e-mails

2. I stopped checking e-mail in the morning and started checking e-mail 3 times a day instead

3. I stopped checking e-mail 3 times a day and decided to check it only once a day

4. I stopped checking and responding to e-mail everyday and decided to check e-mail everyday for important messages and to respond only 3 days a week

Was it easy? No.

Do you have to go to this extreme? No.

But I will tell you I've never been as stress-free as I am now. In fact, it's been exhilarating . . .

Whether you decide to follow my lead or not, do something to get over this awful, time stealing disorder.

Creating Space

Do Not Read Every E-mail

Any idiot can send an e-mail...I should know I send plenty. BUT, that doesn't mean you should read them all.

Weston Lyon

We talked about e-mail before being evil. Here's another lesson about e-mail:

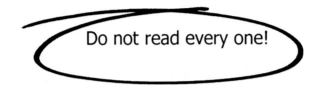

Do not read every one!

I'm sure you get tons of e-mail. I get hundreds a day. And I used to spend all my time reading them. *Wow, what a waste of time!*

Certain e-mails are probably necessary (depending on what you do for a living). Others waste your valuable time.

Eliminate these from your inbox and create tons of time in your life. Don't read them...just delete them!

How do you know which ones?

You already know which ones!

1. Of course, delete the spam.

2. Then delete the ones that raise your blood pressure as soon as you see who they're from.

3. Finally delete the ones that have that stupid **FW:** in front of them.

(Note: If you send tons of e-mail, like me, make sure they ADD VALUE to people. If they don't, then people will delete them without reading them...as well they should!)

Plan Your Errands

Everything is created twice –
first mentally, then physically.

Greg Anderson

Here is another simple, yet effective action that not enough people use. Plan ahead with errands and necessary stops.

Over the weekend, before your week begins, think about tasks that have to be done outside the home during the upcoming week. If they are chores that you cannot delegate, plan how they will be accomplished. Make a list of all the out-of-the-home tasks.

If you are dropping clothing at the cleaners, assemble them and put them in your vehicle. If you are returning movies or library books, put them in bags, label them, and put them in your vehicle. Returns to a store?

Attach the receipt carefully to the bag with a stapler or tape, and, yes, again put them in your vehicle.

Now take your list, and think about your plans for the week. When will you be in the area where the errands have to be done? How can you combine them with work schedules, children's schedules, etc?

Make use of all the times you will be driving right by the cleaners, library, recycling depository, and plan ahead.

This simple ten minute organization can save you time in the morning as you are trying to get out the door to work.

It will save you time, driving back home for all the items you forgot.

It will create space in your day to do fun things like read or relax. **Outstanding!**

It's OK to Say No

No means yes, seriously.

Anonymous

Why do we have so much trouble saying no? And how much trouble do we get into when we can't say no?

Learning to say no can bring us to a great place in our lives. We create more space and more time, which can lead to more energy and happier lives.

We are fearful of saying no for many reasons:

- **We don't want to hurt someone's feelings.**
- **We want to feel needed.**
- **We really want to do it.**
- **We feel bad actually saying it.**
- **We don't want to miss out on something.**
- **We don't want to disappoint.**

But learning to say no more often and at the right times, will enable us to create more time for what is really important in our lives.

By saying **no** to some things, you are saying **YES** to some very important things.

Yes to more time for ourselves. Yes to more time for our health. Yes to more time for what we decide is truly important.

Saying **no** takes practice. A good way to begin is to say it once a day to one request.

Later, you can expand this exercise and start saying no to yourself. **No**, I know I will feel bad if I eat that food. **No**, I know I need my rest more than I need to watch that movie. **No**, soda is not good for me. I will have water instead.

No can be delayed while you get up your courage...

Wait fifteen minutes to give an answer to a request or invitation. Wait one day, if you need that time to practice.

Some of us are so used to saying yes and being agreeable; we have forgotten how to say **no**. Practice.

Remember, saying **no** sometimes is saying **YES** to all sorts of possibilities!

Creating Space

A Place for Everything And Everything in Its Place

I'd lose my head if it weren't attached.

Anonymous

An easy way to create space in your day is to stop wasting time looking for objects. How much time do you waste looking for the same items, every day, over and over? Keys, cell phone, Blackberry, etc.

Decide on a place for these items and always keep them there. Sounds simple, but so many of us do not follow this rule, and we spend way too much time looking for lost items and getting frantic on our way out the door.

Children and students could find one spot for their backpacks and school supplies. Every night, backpacks, lunches and projects can be put in the same place, preferably near the door, so there is no last minute freaking out before the day even begins.

Starting the day in a calm fashion can set the tone for a great day. Feeling organized and together as you leave your home to face the world is a fantastic way to begin your latest adventure in living an outstanding life.

Exercise at Home

Time is your most valuable asset.

Why waste it in the car?

Weston Lyon

Exercising at home will give you, literally, months of your life back.

First, exercising is a **MUST** if you want to create an outstanding life. Without your health, nothing else really matters.

Second, exercising at home saves you hours a week which add up quickly. Let's take a look at this simple, yet astonishing calculation:

Let's say you exercise at your local gym and the gym is 10 minutes away from you. That means you're en route to the gym and from the gym for 20 minutes total.

If you work out only 3 times a week you waste 1 hour of your life every week on drive time.

That's 52 hours of year. And 520 hours every ten years.

That means in a ten-year period you waste over 21 FULL days driving to the gym and back to work out.

Imagine if you just exercised at home? You'd create 52 hours a year of *new* space. And over 21 FULL days of *new* space in a ten year period.

What could you do with that amount of time? **Oy vey!**

(Note: For more information regarding exercising at home check out **www.westonlyon.com**. There you'll find all you've ever wanted and dreamed of in terms of creating the body you desire.)

Exercise with Your Children

A little nonsense now and then
is relished by the wisest men.

Willy Wonka

I can go on and on about the benefits of exercise for you and your child; however let's not focus on that right now. Instead, let's take a look at how exercising with your child will create space in your life.

Exercising with your child allows you to accomplish two important goals at one time. **One**, you're able to spend quality time with your child; and **two**, you're able to get your exercise in for the day while having a great time.

Here are 3 things I love doing with my son that you can take and do or adapt for your child:

1. **Dancing** – My son loves to dance. Unlike his dad he has fantastic rhythm.

   If you've ever danced before, you know its great exercise. And when you add in swinging your child, dipping your child, and lifting your child as you dance you have one terrific, awesome, outstanding exercise session that kicks your butt!

2. **Playing at the Park** – This is one of our favorite activities to do. In fact, when it's spring and summer and you can't find us... *we're at the park.*

Playing at the park isn't just for kids of small stature. It's also for big kids, like me!

You can run, jump, and swing. You can play freeze tag (our favorite), hide and go seek, or whatever your imagination creates.

Have fun. Be a kid. Live!

3. **Using Bodyweight Exercises** – These are my specialty (I've written several books on the subject), so we do a lot of these wherever we go.

Exercises like Pushups, Squats, Lunges, and a slew of other exercises ranging from easy to extremely hard.

Your children will fall in love with these when they see how much fun you're both having. And for an extra bonus, you can make the exercises harder by using your child.

For example, I lift Haven overhead while doing squats – killer workout!

(Note: If this interests you check my website, **www.westonlyon.com**. I'll be releasing a book on this very topic very soon.)

As you can see, we do a lot of exercise in my house. And we have a lot of FUN! Go for it, and write to me with your creative adventures.

(Note: If you don't have kids pass this on to a parent you know...they'll love you for it.)

Creating Space

Get Help!

I not only use all the brains that I have,
but all that I can borrow.

Woodrow Wilson

Whenever my friend Norm Miller is asked, "How can I help you?" he always comes back with: "Well if you know a good psychiatrist..."

That's not what I'm talking about here.

Getting help can come in many forms. Let's take a look at two ways to get help so you can create more space in your life:

Personal Assistants

Personal Assistants can do whatever you need to have done. They can wash clothes. They can cook food. They can take care of the kids when you need a break. They can even go grocery shopping for you!

Think of some things you hate doing. A Personal Assistant may be right for you.

Virtual Assistants

Like Personal Assistants, Virtual Assistants can help you get the mundane tasks done that you don't like to do.

The difference is VA's are invisible. Sort of. VA's are assistants that work out of their own home and you never see them.

They're great if you have tasks that can be done without being present. For example, I use a virtual assistant to post announcements and such on my websites. I can do it, but why waste my time when I can get someone else to do it?

Another thing you can use VA's for is research. Let's say you wanted to research some healthy recipes for your family but didn't have the time. Hire a VA to research for you.

See how easy it is to create time? And it's fun too once you get the hang of it.

Creating Space

Ask for Help!

If I had to do it all over again – I'd get help!

Anonymous

I used to be too proud to ask other people for help. I thought I could do it all. Wow, talk about stressing myself out!

There are too many things to do in this world. And if you don't know which things are more important to you, you're screwed. You'll be stressed out and that's not good.

Luckily, a few years ago I changed my ways. I was listening to Jack Canfield's and Mark Victor Hansen's audio series, *The Aladdin Factor*, and heard them talking about asking for help.

They said, *"You have to A-S-K to G-E-T."*

Yes, they spelled that out. But that made it stick. Hmmm...

You have to A-S-K to G-E-T

You have to "ask to get." If you don't ask for help, then you'll continue to be stressed. If you do ask for help, then you may get the help you need.

I know, I know. What if the person you ask says NO?

Who cares? You'll never know their answer until you ask.

Get used to asking for help. The worst that can happen is you get rejected. No biggie. Ask someone else.

Your time is valuable. You have stuff you want. Create some time in your life by asking for help.

Leverage OPT

To be effective, you must know how to communicate your vision and how to enlist the cooperation of others.

M.Z. Hackman

OPT = Other People's Time

You only have so much time in your day. Why not leverage other people's time to your advantage?

Here's what you do:

1. Make a list of things you have to do
2. Put a star next to the items YOU have to do
3. Put an "X" next to the items other people can do for you
4. Delegate these items to people you work with or family members

Your time is precious. And it should be used to accomplish the tasks that you are the best at; activities that make you money; or activities that please you.

Everything else can be delegated! Everything else can be leveraged using OPT.

Try it. I bet you'll like it.

Enjoy Customer Service

You only get what you give yourself – so give yourself the best.

Dr Robert Anthony

Do you know there are businesses out there that want to serve you?

It's true. I learned this a few years ago from a friend of mine who hates to grocery shop.

We were talking one day when she mentioned, *"I hate to shop!"*

*"**You** hate to shop?"* I asked

"Well, I love shopping for clothes, but I hate shopping for food," she replied. *"That's why I have Sam's Club do all my shopping for me."*

"What do you mean?" I inquired.

She went on to tell me that Sam's Club does her shopping and all she has to do is pick it up and pay the bill. She simply calls their pick-up hotline, gives them her list, and picks it up soon thereafter.

What a service!

And Sam's Club isn't the only business out there that wants to serve you. A friend of mine in Maryland uses a Dry Cleaner that has pick-up and drop-off services.
Talk about saving time!

Check your area for businesses like these that want to serve you. I bet you'll be pleasantly surprised when you start looking.

Again, your time is precious. Don't waste it on errands and chores that other people can do – in this case, WANT to do.

They want your business. Give it to them, so you can live the outstanding life you want to live.

Creating Space

Children and How to Use Them

What do we live for, if it is not to
make life less difficult for each other?

George Eliot

We love them. They are treasures. We would do anything for them. But let's face it. They add to the work load. So let's see how we can turn things around and let our children help us.

A good investment with your time, and to create more space for healthier living, is to teach children to do chores and take responsibility for some housework. This time investment will pay off in dividends.

Children can start when they are small and eager to please. This eagerness to please **does not** always continue into the teen-age years—teach them when they are young!

Here are some ideas to get you started. (You will think of more, I am sure, once you get the hang of it.):

 Little ones can help fold towels and carry things. They can be taught to put away their toys and make their beds. They can learn to set the table and help clear

 Children can be taught to make simple meals. Breakfast is the easiest with cereal and fruit, and they can work their

way up to safely using the toaster. Lunch can be simple sandwiches and later you can teach them simple dinners.

Do not expect perfection

Older children, who can drive, can do errands and grocery shopping. Even those who cannot drive can help with errands. I have hired my fourteen year old daughter to do the grocery shopping and to put away the groceries. All she needs is the ride to and from the grocery store. I gain a couple hours, and she earns money and learns valuable life skills. Win,win!

Many times, as parents, we have the idea that no one can do our job as well as we can, around the house, in the kitchen, and everywhere else. While that fact may be true, who cares?

If you are driving yourself nuts and getting stressed about doing everything perfectly, you are the one who suffers. Lighten up, get help, and use the time you gain to make yourself happier. *Everyone in your life will benefit.*

TEAMwork at Work

Coming together is a beginning;

keeping together is progress;

working together is success.

Henry Ford

Do you know what the word TEAM stands for?

Together

Everyone

Achieves

More

It's TRUE!

Instead of trying to do everything yourself at work, get creative – get a team!

You have strengths and you have weaknesses. And guess what? Everyone you work with has them too.

The beauty is not everyone has the same strengths you have. And not everyone has the same weaknesses you have.

So instead of wasting your time on tasks you hate doing and aren't any good at, get creative. Ask for help from a co-worker and offer to do something they hate to do, but you're good at.

Imagine that? Being a team at work...together everyone achieves more, eh?

Also, work will go faster and you'll enjoy it even more. Creating space doesn't mean creating just creating time...it also means creating time that makes you happy. And when you work on stuff you love, you're in a better mood.

(Note: I realize you may work for someone else and they may not allow this. Let them read this book and then ask them to try it. Who knows...it may work.)

Stop Accepting Every Invitation

When you feel driven to act on
an impulse, take your time to ask if this
is really what is in your best interest.

Eknath Easwaran

Do you really have to accept every invitation that comes your way? Do you really have to go to every networking event you hear about? Is it really that important to be everywhere that other people want you to be?

There are different reasons for attending events or parties. Some of them are valid.

Perhaps it is a networking event, and you truly see some advantages for your business. Perhaps the people that are going to be at a party are people you absolutely love and enjoy being with. Perhaps it is a family gathering and it is truly important to others that you show up.

But sometimes, and more often than we like to admit, we really do not have to attend an event and we do anyway.

Take some time to think. When you receive an invitation or notice of an upcoming event, stop and think:

 Will I regret going/not going?

✔ Will I be too tired the next day to fully participate in my life?

✓ Will it be worth it in terms of work, relationships, and happiness?

✓ Do I truly want to invest my time in this activity?

After thinking about these questions, if you want to go, by all means, go! But if you feel you **have to** do it, analyze those reasons.

Will it *really* hurt someone's feelings, or will she/he care that much? Will there be another opportunity to take part in this activity or is this the only time you can do this?

As far as business, is it important for you to be there?

Many times, we are on automatic and agree to participate in activities that do not help us live outstanding lives. We end up with less sleep, we may overindulge in food or drink, and we may take time away from the people in our lives who are truly important.

Just take the time to think. Remember, how you spend the minutes of your life, is how you spend your life.

Plan Meetings During Lunch *or* On Walks

Why take the journey alone when you can invite others along with you.

Anonymous

You may already do this (congrats if you do), but you can create more space in your life if you have a meeting during your lunch hour.

"Breaking bread" with someone can help you build a great relationship and save you time. And isn't that what life's all about?

Creating magic moments
and memories with people

Also, instead of having a lunch meeting, enjoy a lunch walk.

Just grab a pair of sneakers and go! Not only will you save time and build a great relationship, you'll also get in shape in the process.

It's a win, win, win!

Creating Space

Surprise! You Have to Eat Everyday!

There should not be long stretches between meals. You want to have an honest hunger at each meal. You don't want to be starving.

Diana Fletcher

Planning ahead can make the whole food hassle easier. Some of us like to cook, some of us hate it. Some people don't mind grocery shopping; others dread it and put it off as long as possible.

Many times, we have no time to fix dinner because we are running around like nuts to the next activity, meeting or practice. Whatever our views, a lot of time and stress can be avoided with some simple preparation.

Keep a grocery list on the refrigerator where everyone in the family can write down items as they notice supplies running low.

Some people like having a standard list of necessities they buy every week. They run off copies, leaving spaces to fill in other items. (These can be grouped the way the grocery store is set up so you can follow your list with minimum backtracking.)

Once a week, make your list and at the same time plan dinners and lunches so that you make sure the needed items are on the list.

If you hate shopping, take turns with your partner/spouse, or hire someone to do it (A Personal Assistant...hint-hint, wink-wink, nudge-nudge). If this is not possible, make it as efficient as possible so it takes the minimum of your time.

Planning ahead for the shopping and the food prep creates hours of time a week. One hour on the weekend, working on the list and planning the meals, will give you huge amounts of time later in the week.

Older children can take one turn a week to make dinner. Don't be too picky about what they fix. Soup and sandwiches can be a great meal if someone else prepares it and it gives you time to sit together as a family.

As children grow into this responsibility, they will start planning ahead and helping with the grocery list. If meals are ready to be made, you will find you are not stopping to grab fast food which is so unhealthy and a money waster to boot.

Keep fresh food in the house already washed and ready to go. Make lunches the night before, for you and your children. Keep health food bars in your car, so you always have food handy in times of delays and long appointments.

Try to find recipes to double and freeze. Two meals for the time it takes to make one. A little planning goes a long way.

You have to eat every day. Make it healthy, satisfying and easy.

(Note: Some of these suggestions look familiar? That's because we believe "repetition is the mother of all skill". Take action and ingrain these words of wisdom in your brain.)

Keep Healthy Food Handy

When we don't take a few minutes,
and that is all it takes, to plan ahead,
all we can do is react in ways that don't
lend themselves to healthy living.

Diana Fletcher

If you learn to keep food handy, you'll save a ton of time not to mention a ton of money.

Here are a few ideas to help you keep food handy:

 ## Keep food in your car

You can keep meal replacement bars, a can of nuts, water, and other healthy snacks handy in your car if you plan ahead.

You won't get hungry and feel the urge to stop by your local fast food joint. Think about the time it will save you too.

 ## Keep food at work

You can keep even more food at work. You can keep oatmeal, raisins, nuts, seeds, natural peanut butter, lean meats (if you have a refrigerator), fruits, and much more.

By doing so, you'll be able to eat healthier, while creating time for yourself. Think about it. How much time do you waste at the vending machine or driving to lunch? Use this extra time for yourself – enjoy it.

 Pack your lunch

I carry a cooler with me every day I'm on the road. I bring meal replacement bars, fruit, nuts and raisins, and much more with me.

Doing this keeps me on my eating schedule, while saving me time, money and energy. I don't have to look for a place to eat...I have it with me!

Also, I bring a cooler when I take the kids (my son and his friends) to the park in the summer. Why feed them fast food when we can pack a healthy lunch.

Picnic time, anyone!

Make a list of what healthy foods you can keep handy at these specific places:

In the Car:

1. _____

2. _____

3. _____

At Work:

1. _____

2. _____

3. _____

In a cooler:

1. _____

2. _____

3. _____

The Wonder of Notebooks and Lists

Spinning more plates doesn't increase your talent – it only increases your likelihood of dropping a plate.

Anonymous

How much time do we waste trying to remember things? This time waster could be the biggest space stealer of all.

Trying to remember what we needed at the store, trying to remember what was said at the meeting, trying to remember what someone asked you to bring to the party...not only do we waste time trying to remember, but we then waste time retracing our steps to find the stuff we forgot to bring, and it goes on and on.

Very simple idea: Carry a notebook and...

Write everything down

This doesn't have to be complicated or annoying.

- You jot down the times and dates from the meeting.
- You jot down grocery items as you think of them.
- You jot down errands that you want to do.
- You jot down the woman's name you keep forgetting.

You carry a notebook with you and keep track of your life.

Notebooks come in all sizes, from pocket-size to briefcase size. I suggest smaller, but you have to find what works for you.

Stop wasting time trying to catch up with what you forgot. Let a notebook create some extra space in your day. Use that time for living a better, more outstanding life!

Stop Perfecting

The goal of a winner should be excellence –
not perfection.

Dr. Robert Anthony

I'm not perfect. You're not perfect. And nothing else is ever perfect!

Stop trying to perfect life; it's a waste of time. You'll never achieve perfection and trying to will only drive you buggy.

Here's a phrase to always keep with you:

Good enough...is good enough

I learned this from Dan Kennedy, Direct Response Marketing god. When I heard this, I was a bit stunned. In fact, I didn't really internalize it for several weeks.

Then it hit me. He wasn't saying "don't try your best." He was saying "perfection is not possible, get things done and move on."

Wow! That may sound simple, but that's powerful stuff. Here's a simple example that illustrates getting something done and moving on:

When I wrote my first book, I did some editing. Then I sent it to a friend to edit it some more. When I got it back, I sent it to print. And guess what happened?

The printer said, "Do you know you have some misspellings?"

I said, "I had it edited twice. Just print the thing!"

So why did I tell you this? Because perfection is impossible. If it wasn't the spelling in the book, it may have been the grammar. If it wasn't that, it could have been something else. *Who cares?*

The information in that book (and every book I write for that matter) is way more important than the occasional misspellings and grammatical errors.

Don't shoot for perfection. Just get things done and everything will work out just fine. Remember, good enough is good enough.

Here are several things that I don't worry about at all. I just get 'em done (or have someone else get them done):

- **Washing dishes**
- **Cutting grass**
- **Washing my car**
- **Cleaning my house**
- **Organizing my desk**
- **An much much more**

(Note: I listed these same items when I talked about learning to be lazy. Coincidence? I think not.)

Quick Decisions

The truth is that there is never a really "right time"….there comes a time when one simply hopes for the best, pinches one's nose, and jumps into the abyss. If this were not so, we would not have needed to create the words heroine, hero, or courage.

Clarissa Pinkola Estes

If you want to create an outstanding life you have to learn to make quick decisions.

Will you always be right? No.

But that's life. And the cool thing about being wrong is you learn from the experience. In fact, I've learned way more from my mistakes than I've ever learned from my successes.

Decisions are a part of life. And luckily they're like building a muscle. The more decisions you make, the stronger your decision making muscle gets.

Go make a bunch of decisions today, and see where they take you. Do them quickly as an experiment and find out how good you are. Over time you'll get better and you'll be having a blast with your quick decisions.

(Note: Some decisions do take time to think about, so don't use this advice the wrong way. However, most of your decisions should be made quickly. There are not too many you can't fix if you make a mistake – so go wild and live!)

Stop Talking

Listen to Life, and you will
hear the voice of life crying, Be!

James Dillet Freeman

How much time do you waste with *unproductive talk?*

I am not talking about time with good friends, sharing ideas and parts of our lives that truly interest us. I am talking about useless talk.

Useless talk includes gossiping and obsessive talk. (Going over and over the same old, same old.) Talking about others in a negative way sends out bad energy and never really makes us feel good. Obsessing about the same problems with no eye on the solution is such a time waster.

Sometimes, we talk just to talk, and it helps no one. Going over and over bad stuff only makes us feel worse. Even going over and over good things can tire us out and the people who are forced to listen.

Quiet down and listen. Creating space by quieting our voices can lead to truly rewarding results. You may hear something amazing!

.

Television: The Sneaky Time Stealer

No man's knowledge can
go beyond his experiences.

John Locke

Overall, we watch too much television. We need to take back the time TV viewing is stealing from our lives.

As much as I say I don't like television, I do have some favorite shows and I do watch movies. I have learned various tricks to shorten the time television takes from my daily life.

Enjoy the wonderful benefits of TiVo and recording. You don't really have to watch a show when it is broadcast. Taping it and watching it later can give you back 15 to 20 minutes when you zap the commercials.

Tapes can be watched later when you are on the treadmill or exercise bike. You don't have to give up your shows and movies completely!

Examine what you are really doing when you sit down to watch TV. Is this television viewing really a good way to spend your time? Is it really necessary to have it on every night?

Are those programs really that good that you want to sit there staring in a state of hypnosis?

Pick some shows at the beginning of the week that will really be fun to see and only watch those.

Teach your children to do the same.

People feel that they have to check the news programs every night. No, you don't.

As Gavin de Becker points out in his book <u>Fear Less</u>, the news business is a business. That business seems to be to scare us with fear-promoting TV news. The sensationalized headlines, the threat of terrorism, the pull to come back for more—you might miss something going on!

De Becker points out that if we turn it off, you may find you "are feeling happier, more courageous, more connected to the people you've chosen to have in your life."

He also points out, "If we turn it off, then we can face the important question, which is not how we might die, but rather, how shall we live? And that is up to us."

You can get your information in print or watch the news for *one* telling of the story. You do not have to listen all day.

Limit your television viewing for one week. See if you can have a couple nights with no television at all. You may be very surprised with the results. Notice how much time you suddenly seem to have. You are creating space!

Overestimate Your Time

In life there are no over-achievers,

only under-estimators.

Anonymous

Overestimating time is a lesson I learned from my dad. Like most lessons I learned from him, it took a long time to sink in.

You know what I mean...being young you know everything there is to know, right?

Ha ha! Actually, the older I get, the more I realize how little I know.

Anywho, you can create more space in your life if you overestimate the time you think you need to finish a project. There are two reasons for this:

Projects will always take longer than you think they will.

If you overestimate the time, you will not get time-crunched and ruin other plans you may have made for the day.

2nd **If you miraculously finish early, you have time to spare.**

This time to spare can open up other doors. You can finish other important projects, or you can just relax and enjoy the extra time (wow, what a concept!)

Weston's Rule of Thumb

(actually Erwin Lyon's rule of thumb):

Give yourself 25% more time to finish a project

Creating Space

Welcome the Spaces that are Being Created for You

It is only when we silence the blaring sounds of our existence that we can finally hear the whispers of truth that life reveals to us, as it stands knocking on the doorsteps of our hearts.

K.T. Jong

Learn to recognize the spaces that come naturally in your day. Long drives in the car, waiting in line for coffee, getting to a meeting early...these are all opportunities.

These spaces, or time chunks, are unexpected gifts and instead of getting impatient or mad, we should recognize them as the treasures they are. We have been given extra time!

We can read in while waiting in a line, listen to books on CD in the car, jot down notes for projects while we wait for our dinner date.

We can just sit and *think.* We all need time to slow down. Use these built-in opportunities.

How are You Spending Your Days?

Efficiency is doing things right.

Effectiveness is doing the right things.

Alan Nelson

We have been in a hurry-up mode for so long that it is difficult for many people to figure out how to slow down.

One great way to begin is to look at how you spend your days. Honestly look at how you spend each minute of every day. Often we have developed habits that no longer have any purpose.

Look at your activities and ask yourself, does this activity benefit me anymore? Does it benefit anyone else?

If you are honest with yourself, you will discover many of our activities are unnecessary or could be done by someone else. Eliminating just a few of these unnecessary activities can create extra space in your day.

The purpose of this is **not to immediately fill those moments with more work**. The purpose is to create space to take care of your health. Once you have eliminated time wasters, you can create a life of good health and joy.

How you spend the minutes of each day add up to how you spend your life.

The End...

Now that you have finished reading <u>Creating Space</u>, it's time to go back and review "*How to Use This Book*" on page 3.

Remember, you want harmony and results in your life to make it truly outstanding. Take massive action today and we look forward to hearing from you and/or seeing you at an upcoming event.

We wish you all the best on your journey.
Have an Outstanding Life!

Weston & Diana

Keep Reading ⟹

Creating Space

Claim Your FREE Gifts NOW!

($319 Value)

FREE E-Book

"7 Strategies to Create Time in Your Crazy-Busy Life"
E-book (a $16 value)

FREE Tele-seminar

"7 Strategies to Create Time in Your Crazy-Busy Life"
Tele-seminar (a $79 value)

FREE Special Report

"Mastering the 3 Patterns that Control Your Life"
Confidential Special Report (a $27 value)

FREE Subscription

To our internationally recognized weekly e-zine for
crazy-busy entrepreneurs, Have It All! (a $197 value)

Claim your gifts right now... FREE!

www.CreatingAnOutstandingLife.com

Weston Lyon & Diana Fletcher are the nation's leading experts on helping crazy-busy entrepreneurs have it all - *family, business, and fun!*

Together they have written 4 books:

Creating Space

Fun Re-defined

Don't Stop Now!

7 Steps to Start Living an Outstanding Life

All 4 books are part of the <u>Outstanding Life Series</u> and can be found at:

<u>www.CreatingAnOutstandingLife.com</u>

Books in Print by
Diana Fletcher & Weston Lyon

Creating Space - $17.00

Fun Re-defined - $14.95

Don't Stop Now! - $15.95

7 Steps to Start Living an Outstanding Life- $49.97

All available at **www.CreatingAnOutstandingLife.com**

*****

The Fastest Workout Ever!
$49.97
Available at **www.TheFastestWorkoutEver.com**

The Common Sense Golfer
$24.95
Available at **www.CommonSenseGolfer**

Time Mastery Secrets for Entrepreneurs
$12.95
Available at
www.BookOfSecretsForEntrepreneurs.com

Made in the USA